ANIMALS IN DANGER!

Green Sea Turtles

Nancy Dickmann

BROWN BEAR BOOKS

Published by Brown Bear Books Ltd
4877 N. Circulo Bujia
Tucson, AZ 85718
USA

and

Unit 1/D, Leroy House
436 Essex Rd
London N1 3QP
UK

ISBN 978-1-78121-442-8 (library bound)
ISBN 978-1-78121-464-0 (paperback)

Library of Congress Cataloging-in-Publication Data available on request

Text: Nancy Dickmann
Designer: Supriya Sahai
Design Manager: Keith Davis
Picture Researcher: Laila Torsun
Editorial Director: Lindsey Lowe
Children's Publisher: Anne O'Daly

Manufactured in the United States of America

CPSIA compliance information: Batch#AG/5623

Picture Credits

The photographs in this book are used by permission and through the courtesy of:

Front Cover: Shutterstock: David Carbo.
Alamy: Sergi Garcia Fernandez/Biosphoto 18; Dreamstime: Felis 18–19, Kjersti Joergensen 12–13, Tomi Tenetz 8; Getty Images: Jeff Rotman 14–15, Tumbelaka 16–17; iStock: Vickey Chauhan 4, eriktrampe 8–9, italiansight 10, Joshua McDonough 10–11, N.Nehring 12, Searsie 1, Shane Myers Photo 5, 21; NOAA: 16; Shutterstock: cnfoodfoto 14, David Evison 6–7, rujithai 20.

All other artwork and photography © Brown Bear Books.

t-top, r-right, l-left, c-center, b-bottom

Brown Bear Books has made every attempt to contact the copyright holder. If you have any information please contact: licensing@brownbearbooks.co.uk

Websites

The website addresses in this book were valid at the time of going to press. However, it is possible that contents or addresses may change following publication of this book. No responsibility for any such changes can be accepted by the author or the publisher. Readers should be supervised when they access the Internet.

Words in **bold** appear in the Useful Words on page 23.

Contents

What Are Sea Turtles?

Green sea turtles are a type of reptile. Reptiles breathe air and have scaly skin. Many turtles live on land. But green sea turtles live in water.

Turtles have a shell to protect their bodies.

Green turtles are not really green.
They are usually brownish-black.
They have a layer of green fat under their shell. This is how they get their name.

Habitats and Food

A **habitat** is the place where an animal lives. Green sea turtle habitats are in the oceans. The turtles like warm, shallow water. They often stay near the **coast**. They eat the sea grass that grows there.

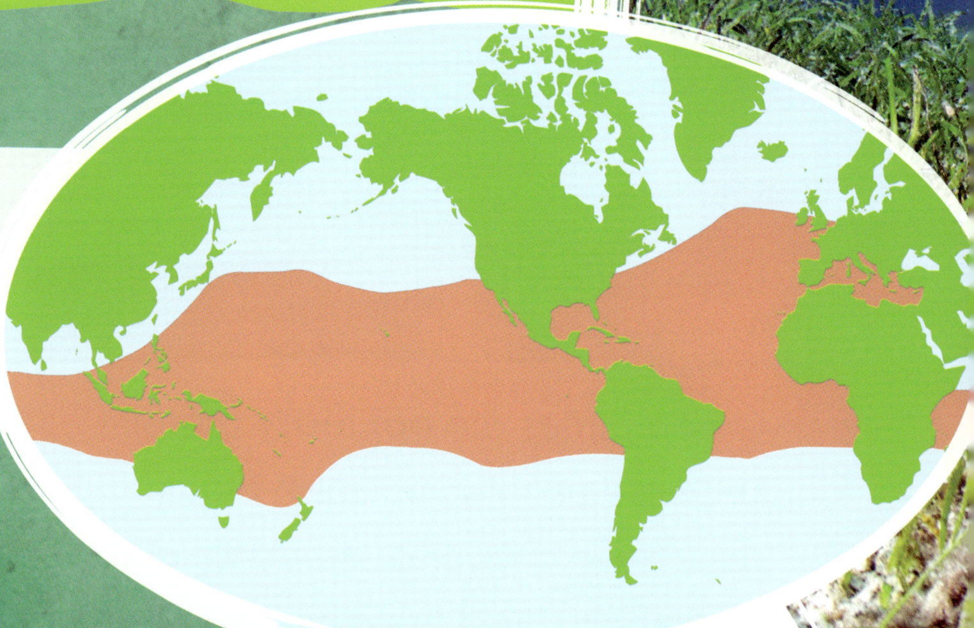

Green sea turtles live in the warmer parts of the world's oceans.

Young green sea turtles eat plants. They also eat small animals, such as worms and jellyfish. Adult green sea turtles only eat plants.

WOW!

Green sea turtles don't have teeth. They have a beak. It helps them scrape **algae** off rocks.

Living Underwater

Green sea turtles are built for life at sea. They have **flippers** instead of legs. This makes them good swimmers. They can see and hear well underwater.

Seawater is salty. Sea turtles get rid of extra salt. It comes out through the turtle's eyes.

Green sea turtles need air. They come to the surface to breathe every few minutes. When they are resting, they can stay underwater for hours.

Amazing Journeys

Female green sea turtles lay eggs. They go back to the beach where they were born. This often means a long journey.

Sea turtle eggs have soft shells.

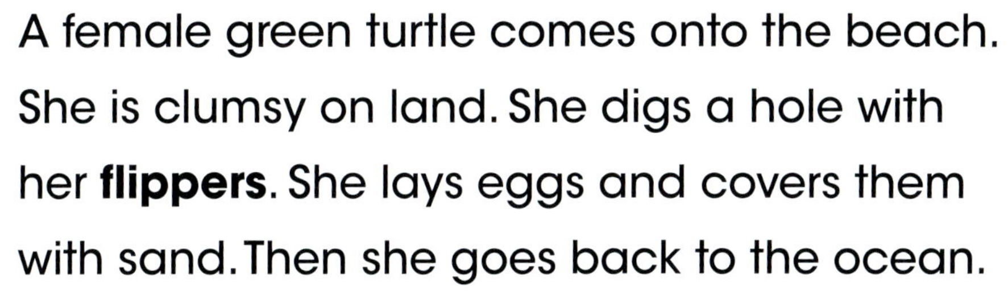

A female green turtle comes onto the beach. She is clumsy on land. She digs a hole with her **flippers**. She lays eggs and covers them with sand. Then she goes back to the ocean.

WOW!

A green turtle can swim more than 1,000 miles (1,600 kilometers) to lay eggs.

Baby Sea Turtles

A baby turtle has a "tooth" on its beak. It helps break the eggshell. The baby turtles dig their way out of the sand. Many **hatchlings** are eaten as soon as they come out.

Crabs and birds hunt the hatchlings.

The other hatchlings race to the sea. Some reach the water. They swim far out to sea. They are safer there.

WOW!

Only 1 in 1,000 baby sea turtles will live to become an adult.

Green Sea Turtles in Danger

Green sea turtles are **endangered**.
People used to catch them for food.
They made soup from their meat.
They ate their eggs.

Green sea turtle soup used to be very popular.

People also caught sea turtles for their skin. It was used to make shoes and handbags. People killed too many turtles.

Helping Sea Turtles

Some boats fish for shrimp. Green sea turtles get caught in their nets. They can't reach the surface to breathe. People are trying to find ways to make fishing safer.

Many fishing nets now have metal **grids**. They keep turtles from being caught.

There are laws to protect green sea turtles. It is often **illegal** to kill them. Beaches and eggs are protected. Rangers protect turtles and eggs.

WOW!

Rangers sometimes collect sea turtle eggs. They take them to a safe place to hatch.

What's Next?

Survival is tough for green sea turtles. Crabs and birds hunt baby turtles. Sharks kill adult turtles. But the main threat is from humans.

Plastic trash floats in the ocean. Sea turtles can get caught in it. They might die if they eat it.

Green sea turtles need safe oceans.
They need safe beaches, too.
People need to protect green sea turtles.

WOW!

Some beaches have signs. They warn people away from turtle nests.

Sea Turtle Helpers

These groups help green sea turtles:

The International Union for Conservation of Nature (IUCN) is a group of scientists. The scientists count animals. They keep track of their numbers. They decide whether an animal is **endangered**. They say when it has gone **extinct**.

The Sea Turtle Conservancy is a charity. It works to keep beaches safe for nesting.

The WWF is a charity. It helps stop people catching turtles or collecting eggs.

Fact File

Average life span: 80 years or more

Size: up to 5 feet (1.5 meters) long

Weight: up to 700 pounds (318 kilograms)

Young turtle diet: eggs, fish, and small sea creatures

Adult turtle diet: algae and sea grasses

WOW!

Many turtles can pull their head back into the shell. Green sea turtles can't do this.

Try It!

Imagine that you are a scientist. You are watching a green sea turtle nest. What happens to the **hatchlings**? Make a pie chart to show the results.

You will need:

- paper
- pencil
- ruler
- compass
- colored pencils

What happens?	Number
egg eaten by dog	10
egg didn't hatch	10
hatchling eaten by a bird	30
hatchling eaten by a crab	20
made it safely to the water	30

1 Use your compass to draw a circle.

2 Use the ruler to divide the circle into 10 "slices". They should each be about the same size. Ask an adult for help doing this.

3 Color in the slices to match the numbers in the chart. For 10, fill in one slice. For 20, fill in two. Use a different color for each group.

Useful Words

algae Small, plant-like living things that live in the water and make their own food.

coast The place where the land meets the sea.

endangered In danger of dying out completely so that no more are left.

extinct Having died out completely so that no more are left.

flipper A wide, flat limb that is used for swimming.

grid Bars that keep large objects from passing through them.

habitat The place where a plant or animal lives.

hatchling A young sea turtle that has just hatched from an egg.

illegal Against the law.

ranger A person whose job is patrolling a park or nature reserve to protect animals.

reptile Member of a group of animals with hard plates or dry, scaly skin covering their body.

Find Out More

Websites

www.nationalgeographic.com/animals/reptiles/g/green-sea-turtle/

www.seaworld.org/en/animal-info/animal-infobooks/sea-turtles

www.worldwildlife.org/species/green-turtle

Books

From Egg to Sea Turtle Lisa Owings, Lerner, 2016

Green Sea Turtle Tom Jackson, Bearport Publishing Company, 2013

The Return of the Green Sea Turtle Melissa Rae Shofner, PowerKids Press, 2017

Index